NORWOOD
A SECOND SELECTION

JOHN COULTER

The History Press

For Relinde

First published 2012
Reprinted 2020

The History Press
97 St George's Place, Cheltenham,
Gloucestershire, GL50 3QB
www.thehistorypress.co.uk

British Library Cataloguing in Publication Data.
A catalogue record for this book is available from the British Library.

ISBN 978 0 7524 6594 4

Typesetting and origination by The History Press
Printed in Great Britain by TJ International Ltd, Padstow, Cornwall.

CONTENTS

All Saints', the parish church of Upper Norwood, 1923.

INTRODUCTION & ACKNOWLEDGEMENTS

Norwood in Old Photographs was brought out in 2002 by Sutton Publishing, now part of the History Press Group. This second volume follows the same pattern, exploring Norwood south to north, from Selhurst Road to Tulse Hill. To simplify comparison between the two volumes, most of the section headings are the same. As Grangewood was exhaustively covered the first time, it has been omitted from this second selection, and Woodside Green introduced in its place. The only other substantial change is the combination of the Beulah Hill and Church Road sections. The commercial north end of Church Road is now included with the Parade and Triangle in chapter 7.

The principle of selection has been novelty. If the reader finds an important landmark missing, the reason will nearly always be that it was dealt with adequately in the first volume. With so many good photographs of fresh roads and buildings clamouring for inclusion, it seemed wasteful to go over old ground unnecessarily.

An innovation has been the inclusion of two maps, which cover nearly the whole area dealt with in the book. Macclesfield Road escapes to the east and Leigham Court Road to the west. The maps are from the early 1920s, slightly later than most of the photographs, to ensure that as many as possible of the places mentioned in the captions can be located on them.

The librarians and archivists of the Croydon Local Studies Library and the Surrey History Centre have been very helpful in settling doubtful points. This time all of the photographs are from my own collection. As before, I have to thank John Seaman for finding some of the best postcards included. Others were pointed out to me by the late, and sadly missed, John Gent.

St Luke's, the parish church of West Norwood, in 1912.

1

SELHURST ROAD & SOUTH NORWOOD HIGH STREET

In 1918 Selhurst Road was still lined almost exclusively with large houses, but this photograph shows two exceptions to this rule. The building with the bell turret was the second South Norwood library. It replaced the first, which was in Station Road, in 1897, and survived until rebuilt in 1967. On the right is the South Norwood branch of the Croydon Polytechnic, now the Samuel Coleridge Taylor Youth Centre.

The fifty-four South Norwood postmen assembled outside the sorting office in Holmesdale Road in this Edwardian photograph look smart and disciplined enough to be soldiers. In a few years many of them were. The sorting office, which was built in 1893–4, is still in use.

The South Norwood Baptist Church in Holmesdale Road was built in 1886 and demolished in 1994. A new church, more attractive than the old (which is not the highest praise), replaced it in 2006.

The South Norwood branch of the Young Women's Christian Association was founded at 241 Selhurst Road a couple of years before this photograph was taken in 1907. These 1860s houses were then being converted into shops one by one. Next door at no. 243 the photographer E. Norton Collins had set up his studio. The houses were part of a car showroom in recent years.

The Pavement was the name for the four purpose-built shops, nos 247 to 253 Selhurst Road, seen here in about 1913. Those of Cornille the gilder and Pearce the electrical engineer were until recently part of the car showroom mentioned above, but the South Western Bank continues, now as Barclays.

The crowd here was watching the South Norwood philanthropist William Stanley drive away after the inauguration of his clock tower on 22 February 1907. The time was 5.20, if the clock was accurate on its first day. It rarely has been since. The pretty tower was a tribute from a grateful suburb on the occasion of Stanley's golden wedding anniversary.

Station Road is seen here from the clock tower in 1912, with Norwood Junction in the distance. The tall building beyond Thomas Butcher's nursery was the South Norwood Public Hall, built in 1866, which was the original home of South Norwood library. The car park of a supermarket now occupies the site.

South Norwood was served by a railway station, the Jolly Sailor in Portland Road, from 1839. The much larger Norwood Junction, its replacement, was built on an open field in 1859, when Station Road was created to provide access to it from Selhurst Road.

This aerial view of South Norwood was taken in the mid-1920s by Surrey Flying Services, a firm based at Croydon Airport. In the bottom left corner is the former South Norwood Public Hall. Eclipsed by the Stanley Halls, it was by this time a furniture warehouse. Norwood Junction dominates the southern half of the picture. The wide railway lines separated the moderately wealthy western half of the suburb from the poorer east, where a number of factories and other industrial buildings can be seen interspersed among the small houses and shops. There the main artery is Portland Road which, emerging from the railway bridge, cuts a straight line across the top of the picture. Branching from Portland Road next to the Signal Hotel (now the Portmanor) is Albert Road. This leads to St Mark's, the parish church of South Norwood, the main feature at the top of the photograph.

South Norwood High Street began to replace Portland Road as the main shopping centre of the suburb after Norwood Junction was opened in 1859. The tradesmen sought to maintain their dominance by the provision of elaborate Christmas decorations. In 1910 they outdid their 1909 effort with these triumphal pillars at the entrance to the High Street from Selhurst Road.

This is nearly the same view as the photograph on p. 13 a decade later, with the addition of Williamson's grocery on the left, at the corner of Oliver Grove. Most of the shops in this southern half of the High Street were purpose-built in the 1860s, but a few earlier cottages survive on the west side, converted into shops.

J. Reeve, hosier and outfitter, had these shops at nos 7a and 8 South Norwood High Street from 1903 to 1917. Since 1999 they have formed two-thirds of the William Stanley public house.

These two photographs of the busy crossroads where South Norwood Hill and Portland Road join the High Street were taken at Christmas 1909 (above) and in about 1914. The fingerpost outside the Albion pub, at the foot of South Norwood Hill, shows all the neighbouring suburbs. Turn left for Upper Norwood and the Crystal Palace, carry on for Anerley and Penge, turn right down Portland Road for Woodside and the Shirley Hills, or retrace your steps for Selhurst and Croydon.

The northern half of South Norwood High Street, seen here at Christmas 1909, was older and less prosperous than the southern half. Some of the cottages on the east side probably predate the railway. That is not the case with The Ship, the main feature on the right, which was built in 1852.

This was the view of the High Street from Goat House Bridge in the late 1920s. The pillar box was outside no. 39, then W.B. Forey's stationery shop and post office. The trams were reduced to a single line at this point, to negotiate the narrow High Street.

2

PORTLAND ROAD
& ENVIRONS

From 1904 we have a series of three photographs of the Portland Road shops, beginning with this one taken from the point where Albert Road branches to the left and Clifford Road to the right. The Home & Colonial Meat Stores were at no. 2, Frederick Durling's greengrocery shop at no. 15.

This was the first group of shops on the south-west side of Portland Road, between Clifford Road and what in 1904 was Farley Road, but is now Doyle Road. R.J. Cornish, the corn merchant, was at no. 2, next door to the Home & Colonial Meat Stores. Lacon's Ales were sold by Thirkettle & Co., the wine merchants at no. 10.

These shops were in the next block on the same side of Portland Road, between Doyle Road and Crowther Road. The nearest was no. 52, the drapery establishment of F. Hughes & Co. That is presumably Mr Hughes at the door. The children were outside Brockman's stationery shop at no. 56. The clock belonged to Ernest Spratt, the watchmaker at no. 62.

Above: Here is the reverse view, towards the bridge from the corners of Farley (now Doyle) Road on the left, and Victoria (now Coventry) Road on the right. The date of this photograph is no longer 1904, but perhaps 1910. The photographer was standing outside the Queen's Arms. The off-licence at no. 47 was the South Norwood Wine Co. The shop on the left, no. 38, was Samuel Brinkworth's discreet pawnbroking business.

Right: W.F. Vincett, the butcher, had his shop at 49 Portland Road, on the south corner of Victoria Road, during most of the 1920s. He succeeded Ernest Robert Vincett, who set up business here in 1913 or 1914. The shop has now been clumsily converted into flats.

The Central Hall Picture Palace in Portland Road, at the corner of Stanger Road, was built in 1910 by James Watt of Catford, to the designs of Edward Stone, also of Catford. They were great cinema pioneers who called most of their creations the Central Hall, usually with as little truth as in this case. The cinema was closed in 1956, but the building survives converted into flats known as Portland Heights.

The Central Hall also features in this photograph, which was taken from outside the Gladstone Arms at no. 167, probably during the First World War. The Croydon Co-operative Stores were at no. 157, at the corner of Apsley Road.

This late 1920s postcard shows the first stretch of the southern half of Portland Road. The Gladstone Arms is in the distance, at the bend. On the left is the Prince of Denmark, an ornate 1898 rebuilding of an 1860s pub. It was recently known as Oceans Apart, but is now closed.

The Gladstone Arms can still be seen in the far distance in this photograph of Portland Road in 1913. It shows the parades of shops on either side of Oakley Road, the turning behind the telegraph pole. They were built in about 1900 to give a foretaste of the architectural horrors the century had in store.

The photographer was standing outside St Luke's Vicarage, at the corner of Grasmere Road, and looking north. This was the last part of Portland Road to be developed. The houses on the right, south of Belmont Road, were built between 1910 and 1912, not long before this photograph was taken.

St Luke's Vicarage in Portland Road was built in 1874. The architect was John Berney of Croydon. It proved too big after the Second World War, when a more modest replacement was provided. Weatherill Court, named in memory of Gertrude Weatherill, mother of the Speaker, Bernard, was built on the site of the old vicarage in 1983.

The development of the fields west of Portland Road was fragmented because the ones in the middle section were attached to Werndee Hall, South Norwood's only country house. When it was rebuilt in 1883, much of the land was put up for sale, and that was when Stanger Road (seen here) was built. This is the view south-west from Crowther Road in 1912.

The 33-acre Enmore Park Estate was laid out in 1855, but builders were slow to move in. Only eleven houses had been completed in Enmore Road by 1868, but they were good, substantial ones, some of which survive. This is the view towards Portland Road in 1910, with the South Norwood Congregational Church, built in 1906, on the right.

Above: Macclesfield Road was built between 1904 and 1908 on part of an old brickfield and adjoining the South Norwood sewage farm. William Edward Prior, who lived at no. 46, was the main developer. William Skinner kept the corner shop at no. 1 from 1914 to 1918.

Left: With so much building in progress all around, Macclesfield Road should have been a good location for a decorator and gas fitter, but T.W. Hollands, whose family is seen here outside no. 68 in 1911, only remained for a year or two.

William Stanley, the great inventor, was a keen amateur architect. He designed this pair of houses, Stanleybury and Cumberlow, nos 74 and 76 Albert Road, in about 1867, and lived at Stanleybury (on the right of this 1907 photo) for ten years. He then moved to the new and much larger Cumberlow at 1 Lancaster Road – also 'my own invention'. Stanleybury and the old Cumberlow were demolished in 2002.

The South Norwood Riding School, which flourished before the First World War, trained its pupils in the field east of Lincoln Road where Hambrook Road, Chartham Road, and Malden Avenue have now been built. The signals seen on the railway embankment in this photograph were at the dividing of the lines to Crystal Palace and Norwood Junction. The school was run by Thomas E. Samson of Penge Road.

The southern half of Manor Road is one of the oldest parts of South Norwood, but the northern end, seen here from Sunny Bank, was built only from 1900. Work was still in progress behind the distant hoarding on the left when this photograph was taken in 1905 or a little earlier.

3

WOODSIDE GREEN

Woodside Green is seen here from its northernmost point, at the entrance to Woodside Avenue, probably in 1908. The photographer was standing at the gate of Woodside Cottage, no. 169, one of the oldest buildings in Norwood.

The north-eastern edge of the green is known as Woodside View. Three of the four houses built there in the 1880s are shown in this Edwardian photograph. On the left is Keith Lodge, now demolished. The other two, Rosslynlee and Rutherglen, were given the numbers 187 and 195 in the 1930s, in anticipation of their being soon replaced by numerous small houses, but they have both survived.

Poplar Farm used to jut out into the green, cutting it almost in two. It was only when it was demolished in 1894 that the present straight south side was defined. These houses were built there soon after. The postcard was sent by a soldier during the First World War.

The green has always been a popular playground for children. This group was gathered near the south-western point, opposite Stroud Road, probably during the early part of the First World War.

This Edwardian snow scene was taken from nearly the same place, the camera just swung a little to the right. The big house was the short-lived no. 92, The Homestead. It was built in the late 1890s and replaced by Cloister Gardens in the 1930s.

Woodside Green comes to a point at its south-western corner, where the two roads join at the entrance to the village. The photograph above shows the view into the village, the other from it. The cattle trough, a favourite rallying point for children, did not enjoy this prominent position for much longer. It was moved to its present site at the junction of Howard Road and Birchanger Road in 1922, and replaced by the war memorial.

The Woodside war memorial was unveiled by the Mayor of Croydon and dedicated by the Vicar of St Luke's on 9 September 1922. The Guard of Honour was provided by the Royal West Surrey Regiment, the South Norwood Silver Band played, and all the local Scouts and Guides were in attendance. The photograph was taken from the Beehive.

These two photographs again show the green from the eastern end of the village, in 1913 above and in 1909 or a little earlier below. The Welford's dairy cart, probably from the Portland Road branch, was outside the shop of William Millest, a baker, at no. 51. The post office was at no. 53. The bottom picture shows the Beehive, a pub founded in 1844. It now has a second storey built over the bars seen here. Selsby Hunt Catterson was landlord from 1880 to 1909.

4

SOUTH NORWOOD
PARK & HILL

This was Lancaster Road, the entrance to the South Norwood Park estate, in the late 1920s.
On the left is part of Ravenscourt, no. 21, a house built in about 1860. The bay window has now been
removed. Beyond it is Felix House, built on the site of the Ravenscourt stables in 1924–5.
The semi-detached houses in the distance, built in 1875, are numbered in different roads. The gabled
house on the right is 82 Warminster Road while the other is 2 Lancaster Road.

South Norwood Park was projected in the late 1850s by Abraham Steer, stove manufacturer, brickmaker, and builder. He was more successful than most Victorian developers, but was still bankrupted twice. These tall houses in Lancaster Road were the second stage of the estate, added in the late 1860s. Most are still standing, including Sombrero House, no. 26, which is seen below in 1911. It was later occupied by William Field, a postcard publisher, but this photograph was probably by one of his rivals.

The asset that placed South Norwood Park above other estates in the district was the Norwood Club. At Norwood Lake, formerly a reservoir of the Croydon Canal, and in the fields around it, a country club had been created, with facilities for all the fashionable sports of the day. The photograph above was taken after Croydon Council assumed responsibility for the lake in the 1930s. It shows a scene of largely unsupervised aquatic fun that the modern child can only dream about. The photograph below shows the cricket ground, tennis courts, and golf course in their Edwardian heyday. Beyond are the mostly demolished houses of Sylvan Road, with the towers of the Crystal Palace peeping over them.

Wesleyan Church, South Norwood.

Above: The South Norwood Wesleyan church, opposite the Stanley Halls, was built in 1874 and demolished in 1977. It is seen here in the early 1920s. On the left is the second South Norwood fire station at no. 9 South Norwood Hill. The brigade moved here from the Albion yard in about 1900 and remained for thirty years. The building was demolished in 2008.

Left: Franklin House, 19 South Norwood Hill, was built in the late 1840s, and originally called 4 Addington Place. It was occupied by John Robertson Reep, a solicitor, when this photograph was taken in 1908. Franklin House was demolished in 2004.

Holmesdale Road begins its long, eventful journey halfway to Croydon at South Norwood Hill, from which this photograph was taken in about 1914. This was the prosperous end of the road, lined with big houses, some of which survive. On the left is the coach house of Albion Tower, 21 South Norwood Hill.

Whitehorse Lane looked unimaginably rural when this photograph was taken, probably just before the First World War. The view is towards South Norwood Hill from the corner of Whitworth Road. The house on the left was Ravenscroft, which was wrecked by a bomb during the Second World War.

The junction of South Norwood Hill and Whitehorse Lane, now a mess of traffic lights, used to feature this cattle trough and elaborate rustic seat. From the tranquil viewing platform the wayfarer could admire the panorama of the Shirley Hills. The houses, 109 South Norwood Hill and its neighbours, are still standing.

Whitehall was built in about 1860 as a pair of houses called The Firs, later 248 and 250 South Norwood Hill. They were combined as a private hotel in the 1890s, and were being used as a nursing home when this photograph was taken in 1909. 'I am mental nursing,' wrote Ella Mackenzie, who sent the card. There is no truth in the legend that Lillie Langtry lived here. Whitehall was demolished in 1974.

Grange Hill used to be one of the most romantic of Norwood's roads, steep, narrow, twisting, and bounded by the leafy gardens of big houses. It is still steep, of course, but its other attractions have been eroded by modern housing developments. This is the view from South Norwood Hill in about 1914.

The Grange, the large house on the right, stands at the junction of Grange Hill and Grange Road, and has lent its name to both. This 1935 photograph also shows the small houses that had just been built in Grange Road on the site of Kingslyn and its garden. Kingslyn Crescent was part of the same development.

The Old Spa House, 249 South Norwood Hill, was one of Upper Norwood's oldest and most important mansions. The first known occupant, in 1803, was Lord Grosvenor, ancestor of the Duke of Westminster. This was the south-west-facing garden front, from which there were wonderful views. The house was replaced by Spa Close, built in 1933.

Beaulieu Heights, 264 South Norwood Hill, has fared better than the Old Spa House, as it survives, divided into flats. There was a house of this name on the site from before 1819, but it was rebuilt in 1861. The house became a Christian Science girls' school in the 1920s (with Joyce Grenfell as the star pupil), but was the Beaulieu Heights Hotel when this photograph was taken in the 1930s.

5

BEULAH HILL & CHURCH ROAD

Mayfield or Red Lodge, 1 Beulah Hill, has stood opposite Church Road since 1883.
This photograph, taken from the garden in 1911, shows the family of Robert Mackay, Principal Clerk
to the General Post Office, who had just moved there. Mayfield was greatly extended on both sides in
the 1980s.

Left: John Sims Reeves (1818–1900), the greatest British tenor of the nineteenth century, was a regular performer at the Crystal Palace. He lived from 1868 to 1896 at Grange Mount, 13 Beulah Hill, a house that stood at the corner of Grange Road until the early 1960s. This photograph, taken at Birmingham, was one of the innumerable cartes-de-visite produced for sale to his fans.

Opposite: Most of the Victorian houses in Highfield Hill have been demolished since the Second World War. If they were all as ugly as Endsleigh, no. 10, that cannot be regarded as a great loss. It was built in about 1868 and originally called Gorway Lodge. The photograph was taken in 1910, when a Mrs Soulby lived here.

The shady, narrow part of Beulah Hill between Grange Road and Spa Hill is seen here during the First World War. The Beulah Spa Hotel is in the distance. The house was Neale Lodge, no. 29, built in 1864–5 and demolished in the early 1960s. These Beulah Hill houses presented their plainer sides to the road, because the garden fronts enjoyed the sun and the view.

This lost Beulah Hill shopping parade was on the opposite side to Neale Lodge, and closer to Harold Road. It was demolished in the 1960s. The postcard was published in 1937 by L.P. Harvey, who ran the post office at no. 18. The Albany cinema, advertised outside, was in Church Road.

Hollybourne, no. 94, was a typical Beulah Hill house, built in the mid-1860s and demolished about a century later, when the original lease expired. It stood opposite The Yews, the surviving no. 77. This photograph was taken in 1910, when Frederick John Nettlefold lived at Hollybourne.

The huge range of flats known as The Woodlands was built in the late 1930s, when this photograph was taken, on the site of an old Beulah Hill mansion of the same name. This might have become the normal housing type in Upper Norwood if the war had not intervened.

This photograph was taken in 1937 from outside Ormesby Court, 124 Beulah Hill, an old house formerly known as Ivy Villa, which had been altered and divided into flats. The houses beyond Queen's Road (now Queen Mary Road) were built in 1926–7.

Gibson's Hill is still the gateway to one of Norwood's most tranquil spots, for around this bend lies Norwood Grove, but since 1914 these hedgerows have given way to rows of houses. The outbuilding on the left belonged to an old mansion called The Rylands.

The Army Service Corps had an important Mechanical Transport Depot at Upper Norwood during the First World War, with its headquarters at Castlehill Lodge, 205 Church Road, now demolished. The men were billeted in empty houses all over the district, but this photograph was almost certainly taken at HQ. The date was 24 January 1919, when most of the men and women of the depot were about to return to civilian life.

Church Road was busy even in 1910, but the traffic was not of a kind to make it unsafe to wheel a pushchair down the middle. This is the view north towards the Triangle, with the rambling Queen's Hotel on the left.

Windermere House, 110 Church Road, was built in 1869 for John George Megaw, and demolished in the 1970s. It was bought by the Royal Normal College for the Blind in 1892 and became the residence of its principals, Sir Francis Campbell and his son Guy. This was the garden front in about 1920. The house on the right was Silverton Lodge, 118 Church Road.

No. 104 Church Road was called Greystoke when this photograph was taken in 1911, but it has had various other names since it was built in the late 1830s. Lansdowne Villa was the earliest and Cambridge House the longest-lived. It is still standing, now used as offices.

6

AUCKLAND ROAD
TO ANERLEY HILL

Fox Hill was part of an old track marking the boundary of Croydon and Penge. This photograph was taken from opposite Tudor Road in about 1918, when there were large detached houses on the south side of Fox Hill, all now gone. The posting box on the right was in the wall of the largest of them, Norbury Lodge.

Auckland Road featured some of the most extravagant Victorian houses in Norwood, a number of which survive. Aucklands, no. 153 (seen on the right in 1937) is still standing, though now converted into flats as Auckland Heights. It was built in the late 1870s for George Normand. Hawkhurst, no. 82, built in the 1880s, is one of the many houses demolished since the Second World War. The woman at the bedroom window was perhaps the German visitor who sent this postcard in 1907.

Right: Mowbray Road shares most of the characteristics of Auckland Road, of which it is an offshoot. It too has lost many of its Victorian houses, including Westerdale, no. 26, seen here in 1932. It was built in the mid-1880s.

Below: The Sylvan Estate was a road of prefabricated houses, or prefabs, one of the thousands laid out after the Second World War to rehouse bombed-out families. It ran from Auckland Road to Maberley Road, in the space between Mowbray Road and Sylvan Road. Sylvan School replaced the prefabs in 1974, but has itself been supplanted by the Harris Crystal Palace Academy.

This is the east end of Sylvan Road, seen from the right-angled junction with Maberley Road. All but one of the old houses on the left or south side have been demolished, but the north side has fared better. Of the four seen here, only the second (Hillside, no. 43) has been lost. Melton or D'Arcy Retreat, no. 45, retains its elevated conservatory.

Most of the Maberley Road houses are on the east side, built on narrow plots hemmed in by the railway. They are therefore smaller and have survived better than their grander neighbours. This is the view north in the 1920s, with Mowbray Road on the left.

The Rising Sun, 72 Anerley Road, is one of Norwood's lost pubs. It was founded in 1851, just before the Crystal Palace moved in next door, and it prospered greatly as a result. Luck ran out during the Second World War, when the pub was wrecked by bombing. The ruin was demolished in the early 1950s. This photograph was taken in the 1920s, when Henry Stephen Bathard was the landlord.

This view down Anerley Hill in the 1920s gives some idea of the steep climb facing the trams labouring up to the Crystal Palace. Ledrington Road is on the left and Cintra Park on the right.

This Edwardian postcard of sinuous Cintra Park shows the present nos 28 to 32. The blue plaque erected at no. 28 in 2010, in honour of Marie Stopes, is wrong in stating that she lived there from 1880 to 1892. The family were at Kenwyn, no. 23, from 1880 to 1882, before moving across the road to Hope House (then no. 8 but now 28) to which they transferred the name Kenwyn.

7

PARADE & TRIANGLE

Only pedestrians with a death-wish stroll across the Crystal Palace Parade today, but before the
First World War it was a fashionable promenade. The building on the left, attached to the High Level
station in Farquhar Road, was the office of the Crystal Palace Coal Co-operative Society.

Left: The Crystal Palace Picture House, the cinema within the great building itself, lasted only from 1920 to 1930 and never equipped itself for showing talkies. This photograph can be dated to 1927 because the British comedy *The Glad Eye*, advertised outside, was released in that year.

Below: The wrong kind of snow had not been discovered when this bleak photograph of the railway cutting was taken from the Parade, probably in the 1920s. The misty outline of the High Level station can be seen on the left. The line closed in 1954 and Spinney Gardens was built here in the 1980s.

Mrs Mary Ann Pedder ran this café in Church Road from 1912 to 1937. It was no. 27 when she moved there but is now no. 79. As the ornate plasterwork on the first floor hints, the shops now 77 to 91 Church Road have an interesting history. They were part of the failed Fellowship Porters' Almshouses, of which the more recognisable relic is now 11 to 25 Belvedere Road. The almshouses were built in 1841, but this range was soon converted into shops as Albert Terrace.

Above: The six shops in Church Road that face Westow Street were numbered 47 to 59 when this photograph was taken in the 1920s, but are now nos 99 to 111. They were built in the late 1850s on the detached tea garden of the White Hart, for its landlord, John Ledger. The pub can be glimpsed on the left, behind the war memorial.

Left: The other edge of the White Hart appears on the right of this picture, which probably dates from 1922, when the Upper Norwood war memorial was unveiled. The view is into Westow Street, and shows the garden of the Royal Normal College. The memorial was moved to Westow Street in 1956.

The house known as The Roses was built in 1875–6 for Joseph Campbell, the Principal of the Royal Normal College for the Blind. It stood behind The Mount, the main building of the college, which can be seen on the right. The Roses was later the residence of the Medical Officer. Both houses were bombed during the Second World War.

This postcard shows Westow Street from the gate of the Royal Normal College in the 1920s. 'Nosegay' was a brand of tobacco sold by S.C. Greenhill at no. 70. The Temperance Billiard Hall was at no. 68. These shops and the college have been replaced by the supermarket.

These two photos of Westow Street were taken from the north or Central Hill end, before 1910 above, and in the 1920s. This was the second best shopping street of the Triangle, and it seems to have declined during these fifteen years. Both pictures show the clock outside Gaydon & Sons, the watchmakers, at nos 16 and 18. It now adorns the Foresters' Hall, on the opposite side of the road. In the distance is the spire of St Andrew's Presbyterian Church, now the Greek Orthodox Church of Saints Constantine and Helen.

This photograph shows the western end of Westow Hill, with the corner of Gipsy Hill in the distance. On the right is the Queen's Arms at no. 23, and beyond it the gates of the Upper Norwood Wesleyan Church, now replaced by a supermarket. The date is before 1906, as Cooper the bootmaker had gone from no. 17 by then. James Chittell was a fishmonger at 74 Westow Street.

James Morter set himself up as a butcher at 49 and 51 Westow Hill at the beginning of the 1880s. The business prospered, and by 1910 had reached the impressive scale seen here, when it occupied nos 45 to 51. It contracted in the late 1920s, but was still trading in 1939 as a fishmonger's shop and restaurant at nos 45 and 47.

This was the central section of Westow Hill in the 1920s. Part of Barclays Bank, no. 61, can be seen on the right, with the entrance to Woodland Road beyond it. On the left is the Woodman pub at no. 56.

The eastern end of Westow Street, seen here from the corner of Church Road in about 1914, is little changed today. The Cambridge Hotel has closed, but most of the shops remain intact, though the building on the right is no longer a bank.

8

CENTRAL HILL
& ENVIRONS

Hawke Road survives as the name of a service road on the Central Hill Estate, but all its original early 1880s houses have been demolished. This 1920s view from Victoria Road towards Roman Road was probably taken on a Sunday morning.

It is curious that these two postcards of Crown Hill were wrongly identified by their publishers. The photograph above, taken from Crown Point in 1937, was captioned 'Knight's Hill', and the other, taken halfway down in the early 1920s, was called 'Central Hill'. It shows St Wilfrid's Cottage on the right, the convent in the distance, floating above the trees like a dream palace, and on the left the hoardings behind which the southern end of Tivoli Road was being built. Crown Hill was changing at this time, with the loss of houses to shops and flats, and the introduction of unsympathetic street lighting, but the ultimate insult – the alteration of its name to Crown Dale – was still two years away in 1937.

The bottom of Central Hill was extraordinarily open, almost rural, when this aerial photograph was taken in the mid-1920s. West of Hermitage Road (which runs across the bottom of the picture) was the Convent of the Faithful Virgin, with its extensive grounds. The trees on the right were in the garden of Bloomfield Hall, soon to be replaced by a council estate, and Norwood Park can be seen in the distance.

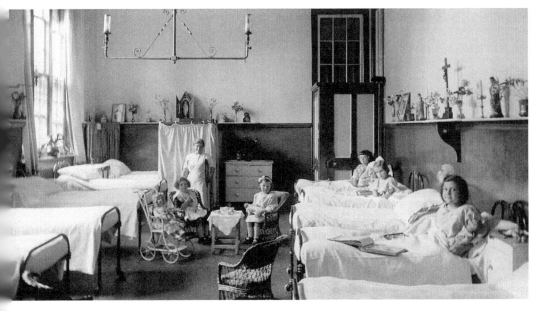

The main worldly work of the convent was the upbringing and education of orphan girls. Some of them, looking cheerful enough, are seen here in the infirmary, during the 1920s.

The Norwood Cottage Hospital in Hermitage Road, which was designed by J. & J. Belcher, opened in 1882. A wing added in 1893 was the first of several extensions. The hospital was closed in 1984, but the building survives, horribly altered, as Canterbury House.

The cottage hospital soldiered on, heavily sandbagged, throughout the Second World War, during which these three nurses added Air Raid Precautions duties to their many other tasks.

This photograph of Lunham Road was taken from the corner of Hawke Road, probably in 1913. It has not fared quite so badly as Hawke Road, as the houses on the left survive. The house framed by the end of the road was The Highlands (otherwise known as Heraklea or Saxawald), a fine Gipsy Hill mansion with grounds allegedly landscaped by Sir Joseph Paxton. It was replaced by Highland Court in the 1930s.

Highland Road has been nearly extinguished: only the houses seen in the distance in this 1913 view have survived. This main section has been renamed Vicars Oak Road, and is now lined with small modern houses. The gate on the right was the back entrance to 12 Central Hill.

Margaret Lockwood (1916–90), the most popular British film star of the 1940s, was born in Karachi, but lived in Upper Norwood with her awful mother from 1920 until her marriage in 1937. Their home during most of that time was 18a Highland Road, part of an 1870s house called Byculla. It was destroyed during the Second World War.

Aristocratic All Saints' established a mission hall in Norwood New Town, its local slum, in 1895. In 1903 this permanent mission church was built in Chevening Road, on the edge of New Town, and named St Margaret's. Its permanency is now in serious doubt, as it has been closed for ten years and lies derelict.

St Margaret's can also be seen on the left of this photograph taken from the Upper Norwood Recreation Ground. This park, which is better known as the Harold Road Rec., was opened in 1890. The large building seen above the now-demolished bandstand is the Queen's Hotel in Church Road.

St Andrew's, or Wynfrith, the present 30 Harold Road, was numbered 18 when this photograph was taken in about 1910. The house was then occupied by Colonel John F. Worlledge. It was built in the early 1890s, and is almost restrained in comparison with the later houses in this road of competitive architectural display.

Bedwardine Road continued the architectural style set in Harold Road, from which this photograph was taken in the 1920s. At that time four of these houses were used as annexes by the Royal Normal College for the Blind in Westow Hill, the grounds of which ran down to Bedwardine Road. Only half of the houses seen here survive.

9

GIPSY HILL &
DULWICH WOOD

The dramatic view down Gipsy Hill was sadly hazy when this Edwardian photograph was taken. The houses on the left, Esslemont and Derwent House, nos 19 and 21, are still standing. They were probably built for Robert Canham, a Westow Street ironmonger, who lived at no. 17. The tower of Christ Church survives, but the body of the church was destroyed by fire in 1982.

Walter John Garnham was a builder and decorator at 29 Woodland Hill from 1909 until the early 1920s, while his wife May ran a general shop as a sideline. When this photograph was taken Walter had retired from building and settled down to semi-retirement behind the counter. The shop, on the north side, near Woodland Road, just survived the war, but was demolished afterwards. Paxton Primary School is on the site.

The photographer chose a damp day to record this scene at Gipsy Hill station just before the First World War. He was standing at the corner of Colby Road, with Merlin Broom's bakery at no. 130 on his left. This being Upper Norwood, the street boys were better dressed than usual and, with one exception, better behaved.

Robert Webster ran this smart grocery shop at 124 Gipsy Hill, directly opposite the station entrance, from 1906 or a little earlier until the Second World War. This photograph was taken near the start of that period, and presumably shows Mr and Mrs Webster at the door. The shop is now a fostering resource centre.

The north end of Gipsy Hill had almost the air of a London square, with the largest houses in the road facing the equally luxurious properties in Dulwich Wood Avenue across an enclosure of grass and trees. By no means all the houses survive today, but the green is still there, in an unkempt condition. It was sometimes called the Triangle and sometimes French's Field, after the Gipsy Hill dairyman whose cows can be seen grazing it in the picture below, but is now known as Long Meadow. It is on the right in the top photograph, which was taken in about 1920, somewhat later than the other.

A good run of large late Victorian houses still lines the Gipsy Hill side of the meadow, but the largest ones have been demolished since the Second World War. They include the two seen here in photographs from about 1920. The Nook, 101 Gipsy Hill (above), which stood well back from the road, was built in the early 1880s on the site of Gipsy House, one of the early Norwood mansions. The Nook was later known as Charters, and Charters Close is the name of the modern development on the site. Grazeley, 107 Gipsy Hill (below), a house of the late 1870s, has been replaced by Grazeley Court.

Above: Ravenstone, 61 Farquhar Road, was a boarding house created by linking two detached 1870 villas with the three-storey block seen in this 1916 photograph. The first occupants of the nearer house, The Ferns, were Samuel Carter Hall and his wife Anna Maria, both writers, often in collaboration. Glenmare House was the other half. Ravenstone was demolished in 1973 or soon after.

Left: Leslie Howard (1893–1943), Norwood's second great gift to British cinema, emerged from another boarding house. His father, Ferdinand Steiner, let apartments first at 45 Farquhar Road, then at 4 Jasper Road. Howard got his early experience with the Upper Norwood Dramatic Club, which was founded by his mother.

Kingswood Drive began as Church Walk, became Church Road, and was known as Kingswood Road from the time when houses began to appear in the early 1870s, until 1938. The houses, all but one demolished, were large and luxurious. Grovehurst, no. 8, seen above in 1911, is the only survivor. Beaumont, no. 1, was a hall of residence for the Gipsy Hill Training College in the 1920s, when the photograph below was taken in the front garden. It was demolished in the early 1950s.

Only a few of the splendid 1860s houses of Dulwich Wood Avenue still survive, and no. 34 is not among them. It was originally called Woodlands, but was occupied for sixty-five years by the Rehder family – among the many German settlers near the Crystal Palace – and they renamed it Lubeck House. This was their Christmas card in 1913. Lubeck House was destroyed late in the Second World War.

Dulwich Wood Avenue, originally just The Avenue, is seen here from the north end, where seven roads meet at the boundary of Upper Norwood, West Norwood, and Dulwich. The building on the left was the Gothic red-brick stable block belonging to the Italianate house called Homedale, 44 Dulwich Wood Avenue.

10

GIPSY ROAD
& DISTRICT

Dulwich Wood Park is seen here from Gipsy Road in 1911 or a little earlier. The Paxton Hotel (now closed) is on the left and in the distance Avenue Gate, a pair of houses that occupied a prominent position at this important junction until they were bombed during the Second World War.

This photograph was taken at about the same time as the last from some fifty yards further back. It shows the entrance to Hamilton Road on the left, with Jesse Skinner's off-licence at the corner, and the gates of the Gipsy Road Baptist Church on the right.

In this reverse view from the 1920s, the Paxton Hotel is on the right and the Baptist Chapel in the distance on the left. The Sayer & Bodkin shop seen on the opposite page was in the terrace on the left.

This shop at 232 Gipsy Road was in the fancy drapery line long before Sayer & Bodkin took it over in 1923. They only remained for a few years, but other drapers succeeded them. It is now an Indian restaurant, with only one door, dead centre.

These early 1920s photographs show the two schools in Gipsy Road. Above, the rear of Salter's Hill School is seen from Norwood Park, with the railway running between. It was opened in 1880 and is now Kingswood Primary School. The bottom picture shows the Gipsy Road school on the left. It began as an offshoot from the Congregational Church in Chapel Road. The Gipsy Road building was opened in 1875, but had been much altered and enlarged when this photograph was taken. After many changes of name and use the taller surviving part is now the Kingswood Primary School Lower Site.

These houses stood on the outside of the first bend in Hamilton Road, where it swings towards Clive Road. The detached house on the left, no. 133, looks much the same today, but the rest have been rebuilt. Christopher Laflin, the tailor, lived at no. 137.

This photographer was standing at the second bend in Hamilton Road, outside the almshouses, and looking north towards a distant Carnac Street. Many of these pleasant 1850s cottages have survived.

The St Saviour's Almshouses, built in 1863 and enlarged several times, were a combination of Southwark charities robbed of their ancient sites by the growth of the Victorian railways. They were restored after serious bomb damage in the Second World War, but have recently been demolished (except for the chapel) and replaced by Tannoy Square. This was the view from the Hamilton Road entrance in 1906.

Nicholas Ley acquired this dairy at 232 Rommany Road at the beginning of the First World War and it was continued into the 1930s by his daughter Annie. The premises were shared with the West Norwood Conservative and Unionist Workmen's Club. Flats called Robert Gerrard House are now on the site.

11

ELDER ROAD & NORWOOD HIGH STREET

The Crystal Palace dominated the Norwood skyline and was especially dramatic when seen across the Gipsy Hill valley. This photograph was taken from Norwood Park, soon after it opened in 1911. The Palace was asymmetrical because the north transept was lost to fire as early as 1867.

The site of the western half of Norwood Park was occupied by three smallholdings until 1909. Two of the houses were then demolished, but the middle one, Boundary Cottage, was retained as a picturesque feature when the park opened in 1911. These children were pictured playing outside it soon afterwards. Boundary Cottage burned down in 1942.

The northernmost of the smallholdings was known as Cutting's Cottage after the last tenant, John Cutting, a cow keeper. Like the similar Boundary Cottage, it was built in 1812. This photograph, taken in 1909, shortly before the cottage was demolished, shows Margy and Fred Cutting.

The London County Council did not add many municipal features when it laid out Norwood Park between 1909 and 1911, but it did exploit the natural advantages of the hill by creating this imaginative viewing platform, now long gone. The photograph was taken in 1913.

The original pond at Norwood Park is seen here in 1913, with the viewing platform in the background. It fell into disrepair in the early 1970s and was replaced by a paddling pool cum cycling and skate-boarding area in 1980. It is now dry, yet another symptom of municipal hydrophobia.

This mid-1920s aerial view shows the massive extension to the Lambeth Industrial Schools in Elder Road designed by Edward Buckmaster Coe, and built in 1883–4. The school was founded in 1810 at the southern end of Elder Road, where today the only surviving buildings are to be found. It was a self-contained community, with its own dormitories, chapel (bottom left), laundry (top left, opposite Dassett Road), and out of this picture its own infirmary, swimming bath, and even a large fish pond. All the Buckmaster Coe buildings were demolished between 1966 and 1975. The 1920s Lambeth council houses at the top of the picture still survive, as do the St Luke's church school on the right, at the corner of Linton Grove, and the former St Luke's parish hall (now an evangelical church) standing isolated amid the allotments on the east side of Elder Road. The allotments were intended to be an addition to Norwood Park, but the gardeners obtained a reprieve, and eventually Norwood Park Road and Eylewood Road were built there instead.

William James Watford had this greengrocery shop on the south side of Chapel Road, just east of Ladas Road, from 1905 until the First World War. It was known as 6 The Pavement because these shops were a late addition to Chapel Road, built in 1895 after the main numbering sequence was established. This photograph was taken in 1906. The shop is now a house.

Ash Villas were built in 1880–1 on the east side of Norwood High Street, just north of Gipsy Road, and were soon numbered 151 to 165. They are still houses, an unusual feature in a street otherwise given over almost entirely to shops.

Ash Villas can just be seen lying back from the shops on the right in this second Edwardian postcard which shows nearly the whole length of Norwood High Street from its southern end. The elaborate white canopy adorned the shop of Frederick Griffiths at 120. The canopy has gone, but the shop is still occupied by a butcher.

This 1920s photograph of the High Street shows the same view towards the railway bridge as the last, but from 100 yards closer. No writer on Norwood can fail to be moved by the 'Wilson' sign at 103 on the right. James Benson Wilson, undertaker and antiquary, wrote the invaluable *Story of Norwood*, which preserves much of the suburb's oral history. His family had run this business for generations.

The original West Norwood fire station in the High Street was built in 1881 and replaced by the Norwood Road station in 1914. St Luke's Church next door acquired it as a parish hall in 1917, and since 1969 it has been the South London Theatre Centre.

This brave attempt to squeeze a department store into a small shop began in the 1870s as the Norwood branch of the Brixton Co-operative Society, and continued into the 1930s. This photograph was taken in 1906, from the High Street. The address was then 36 Auckland Hill, but the building, greatly altered, is now no. 120.

Auckland Hill is seen here in 1911 from opposite the Co-operative Stores. The Down platform of West Norwood station is on the right and the Auckland Hall on the left. The hall (now demolished) was an evangelical church founded by Thomas Wilberforce Stoughton, the publisher. Many Hodder & Stoughton employees were recruited from the congregation.

This dramatic view down Auckland Hill was popular with artists and photographers. In the far distance the Jews' Hospital in Knight's Hill appears to be enveloped in smoke, but I think it is only a blemish on the negative. The date is about 1910.

The ladies and gentlemen of the West Norwood Cycling Club were photographed in 1906, almost certainly in the garden of Aucklands, 14 Auckland Hill, which was the club's headquarters. It was also, from 1902, the home and works of the Crisp Brothers, makers of the Retreat bicycle, who were the sponsors of the club. Their cycle was named after The Retreat, 3 Pilgrim Hill (a house demolished in 1999–2000) which was the home of the Crisp family before they moved to Aucklands. Shortly before 1914 the firm moved again, to 72 Norwood High Street, and there they remained until after the death of the last surviving Crisp brother in 1966. By that time they were concentrating on the sale and repair of motorbikes. The cycling club vanishes from the local directories during the First World War, in which many of its members doubtless perished.

12

KNIGHT'S HILL &
THE STREATHAM BORDERS

The main feature of this mid-1920s aerial view of Crown Lane is the British Home and Hospital for Incurables, which was built in 1894. To the right of the hospital is the old Rose and Crown pub, which was destroyed by a bomb in 1940 and not rebuilt until 1957. It is now a supermarket. To the left are the two huge houses called Pierrepoint (closest to the hospital) and Boscobel. They were built in the late 1870s and replaced by a new wing of the hospital in 1939. In the foreground are the Metropolitan Water Board reservoir and William Rockingham's nursery.

Casewick Road, named after a village in Lincolnshire, was laid out in the early 1880s, but developed slowly. There were only thirteen houses in 1894, but many more had been built when this photograph was taken just before the First World War. The turning on the right was then a detached part of Thurlby Road, but since 1981 it has been called Tredwell Road.

Thornlaw Road was named in 1878, and building began at the Knight's Hill end in 1882–3. This is the view up the hill from the Casewick Road junction in the 1920s.

Hill Brow was no. 91 Leigham Court Road when this photograph was taken from the garden in 1909, but it was later renumbered 317. George Henry Shepherd and his wife sent out the picture (which features Mrs Shepherd and her dog) as a Christmas card. Hill Brow was built in the 1860s and demolished in the 1950s, a typical lifespan for a Victorian villa in Norwood.

Selsdon Road was named in 1880, but as with the other roads on the St John's Farm estate, development was slow and patchy. Only half the houses had been built, in isolated groups, by 1894. In this Edwardian view from Wolfington Road the different ages of the houses are suggested by the growth of the creepers.

The top of Knight's Hill looked very different in 1937, because after the war the old shops on the right were demolished and replaced by new ones set back behind a green. The two small shops on the left have also gone, but the terrace of three survives. This postcard was published by S. Ascott of the post office (see below).

The publishing of postcards was a tradition at the Knight's Hill post office. Frederick Hedger, seen in the doorway here, produced this and numerous other Norwood cards, some of which can be seen in his window display. The date was probably 1906, soon after which the number of the shop was changed to 268. Hedger was here for thirty years from 1905.

This photograph of Knight's Hill from near the top was probably taken in 1926. The Lambeth council houses on the right had recently been built on the site of Holderness House, the home of the eminent engineer Thomas Henry Maudslay. The ones on the near (or uphill) side of Furneaux Avenue were destroyed during the Second World War and replaced by Cooper House.

The land known as Holderness House meadow was saved from the hands of builders by a local committee that raised most of the £1,250 price. The London County Council and Lambeth Council paid the rest, and the committee laid out the meadow as Knight's Hill Recreation Ground in 1914. It is now Tivoli Park. This is the view down the hill to the 1920s council houses in Tivoli Road.

Knight's Hill House, built in the 1850s and later known as Lyndhurst and Millburn House, became the Lambeth Council Maternity Home in 1926 – this looks like an opening day photograph – and was later a hostel. It was demolished in 1990, but already the sheltered housing that replaced it is empty, and there are plans for a new fire station here at 210 Knight's Hill.

The view up Knight's Hill from St Julian's Farm Road is very different today, with all these buildings demolished and the scene dominated by the bus garage. In 1913 the main feature was the police station, which occupied 59 Knight's Hill, an old cottage, from the 1870s until the 1930s. A file of bobbies can be seen setting out from it on their beats.

In 1923 the booking hall of West Norwood station was in the news because the young clerk posing nervously on the right was held up by three armed robbers at midnight on 18 January. The thieves took £30 from the till and – to add insult to injury – made their escape by train without even buying tickets.

The main features in this 1910 view of Knight's Hill are West Norwood station, which opened in 1856, the Norwood Hotel, which was built seven years later to take advantage of the railway trade, and on the right the great gates of the Jews' Hospital, built 1861–3.

St Luke's dominates this mid-1920s aerial photograph, but there are other points of interest. Bottom right is the old Horns Tavern, on the edge of the railway cutting, and bottom left the old public library, still standing proudly today while its modern replacement is a ruin. Top right are the small houses, now mostly demolished, of Dunbar Street and Wood Street, and top left the even smaller houses of the great majority sleeping in West Norwood Cemetery.

13

NORWOOD ROAD & THE DULWICH BORDERS

The West Norwood Cemetery, opened in 1837, was one of several intended to replace the insanitary inner London graveyards. It contains an amazing collection of listed structures, but they are nearly all tombs. Sir William Tite's two chapels have both been destroyed. The one seen here was the Church of England chapel, which was demolished in 1955 following bomb damage during the war.

Robson Road was created with the cemetery, of which it forms the northern edge. It was considered part of Park (now Park Hall) Road until 1903, when it was renamed in honour of William Robson, the first superintendent of the cemetery, but it was known locally as Cemetery Wall. These 1880s cottages, called Oxford Terrace, were the first houses in the road.

Bloom Grove, a development of the 1860s, is the nearest West Norwood gets to the contemporary square and garden town planning of Notting Hill and Earls Court. This Edwardian photograph shows the west side, with the green on the right and the railway line in the background. These were the first houses built, in 1865.

Monumental masons and florists always clustered round cemeteries. George Henry James had his shop at 216 (later 376) Norwood Road, nearly opposite the cemetery gates, from the 1880s to the 1930s, and it is still occupied by a florist. James also ran the Castle Nursery on the south side of Canterbury Grove. It was on the site of Castle House, a huge castellated school demolished in the 1850s.

This was the south end of Norwood Road in 1909 or a little earlier, with St Luke's Church in the distance. The London and South Western Bank at the corner of Chestnut Road is now Barclays. Lansdowne Hill is on the right. Disappointingly, the Wright Brothers did not sell aeroplanes, but ladies' underwear.

The Lansdowne Hall, at the foot of Lansdowne Hill, is an evangelical church founded in 1892. The main church building replaced the original iron tabernacle in 1907, and is seen here soon after. It was burned out in 1944, but restored in the 1950s. The little lecture hall on the right was built in 1897.

Just up from the Lansdowne Hall, beyond Canterbury Grove, Henry Barker kept this humble general shop at 9 Lansdowne Hill from the late 1880s until 1923, when he took to dealing in furniture. These cottages were demolished after the Second World War.

The large houses that once lined the west side of Norwood Road became building sites after 1918. When the top photograph was taken, probably in 1926, the hoardings nearly opposite Chatsworth Road were promising a new West Norwood Public Hall, presumably to replace the one in Knight's Hill, which had recently closed. What West Norwood got instead was the Regal cinema, which was opened in 1929. It is seen below in the spring of 1937. The Regal closed in 1964, and after a session as a bingo hall, was demolished in about 1981.

The triangle enclosed by Norwood Road, York Hill and the railway line was occupied until the 1890s by a dozen large houses and their gardens. In 1895 a development scheme was concocted, the largest of the houses were demolished, and three new streets were created. The major ones were Harpenden Road, seen above in 1918, and Ullswater Road (originally Ullswater Street), seen below in 1911. Harpenden Road featured only dull 1890s houses. Ullswater Road was enlivened by the Anglo-German School of Music, on the right in this picture, and on the left by the flats called St Martin's Mansions, and by the Willoughby Hall, outside which the two boys were standing.

Chestnut Road, one of the key elements in the development of the Thurlow Park estate, was laid out i 1848, and in 1849 *The Times* recorded that 'villa residences of a superior description are in course c erection' there. These were the houses known as Park Villas, several of which survive on the south side Some are seen on the right in this 1912 view.

Park Hall Road, which was known as Park Road until 1939, is wide and handsome at its Dulwich enc but narrows in this curving section that leads to Norwood. The West Dulwich Congregational Church at the corner of Chancellor Grove, was built in 1855. It was bombed in 1940 and rebuilt as a Methodis church, but is now a day nursery.

In the prosperous Victorian suburbs the nonconformist ministers were often men of power and influence, and sometimes of considerable wealth. Archibald Geikie Brown (1844–1922) who was pastor of the Chatsworth Road Baptist Church from 1897 to 1907, lived in some style at the distinctive house known to him as Tredegar, but to us as Gothic Lodge, 21 Idmiston Road. It was there that this photograph was presumably taken. It was issued as a commercial postcard to be sold to Brown's many admirers. He left Norwood to become minister of the Metropolitan Tabernacle at the Elephant and Castle.

The north end of Ardlui Road was laid out in the 1860s as Balstone Road, but nothing happened for forty years until the name was changed to Ardlui Road in 1904, and an extension was built south of Idmiston Road. The top picture shows the new southern section a few years later. The view is towards Chestnut Road, with the episcopal chapel of the cemetery (see p. 103) in the background. The most distant house on the left in the top picture is 2 Ardlui Road, which is seen below in 1909. The boy was presumably the son of George Fairman, the occupant at the time. The card was sent 'with Alfred's love', Alfred being the rabbit.

Lancaster Road, now Lancaster Avenue, has been one of West Norwood's best addresses since the first houses were built on the south side in the 1850s. Lancaster Villas was the original name for this group of 1860s semi-detached houses on the north side. The nearest one, no. 13, was destroyed in the Second World War. This photograph was taken in 1907.

Thurlow Park Road, seen here in about 1914, was projected in the 1840s, but building did not begin seriously until the 1860s. St Cuthbert's English Presbyterian Church, at the corner of Court (now Elmcourt) Road, was founded in a temporary building in 1894. The permanent church seen here was built in 1901. It closed in 1990, and is now the Rosemead Preparatory School.

All the houses on the east side of Rosendale Road between Park Hall Road and Elmworth Grove have been demolished. The tall ones (nos 74 to 78) were no loss, but the early 1850s pairs beyond were similar to the much-loved Thurlow Villas, around the corner in Park Hall Road. They all survived the war, but have been gobbled up since by Cormorant Court.

All Saints' in Rosendale Road, one of the grandest churches in South London, has also been one of the unluckiest. It was built in 1887–91, to the designs of George Fellowes Prynne, severely damaged in the Second World War, and restored in 1952 by Norwood's greatest architect, Ninian Comper. In 2000 a fire destroyed the interior and the roof, but the church has now been restored again. This photograph was taken in 1914.

14

TULSE HILL
& ENVIRONS

Palace Road is one of several that begin in Norwood but climb up and over the hill into Streatham or Brixton. It was first proposed in 1810 and was known as Green Lane until the arrival of the Crystal Palace gave it a new name and encouraged the building of the first houses. This is the Norwood end in 1906, with Probyn Road on the right.

These two postcards, from 1913 above and 1905 below, show the section of Norwood Road between the railway bridge and Approach Road, which leads to Tulse Hill station. Motor buses had ousted the horse-drawn ones between those dates. On the right of the top picture are the lock-up shops that then occupied the whole space where there is now a footpath to the station. The advertisements on the wall above them were aimed at the railway more than the road. On the left of the bottom picture can be seen the walls and gates of the Roupell Park Wesleyan Church, which stood opposite Approach Road until 1969. The tall Victorian shops still survive on both side of Norwood Road.

Perran Road was built in the early 1880s across the garden of Tulse Dale, the large house that stood until then at the corner of Norwood Road and Tulse Hill. It was a quiet backwater when Charles and Ellen Coborn were photographed at the gate of no. 40 in 1911, but since then its peace has been disturbed by the building of Hardel Rise and the creation of the one-way system. The house survives, minus the creeper.

Above: This 1905 view of Norwood Road from the corner of Thurlow Park Road shows the spire of the Roupell Park Wesleyan Church and (behind the lamp post) the entrance to Perran Road. The shops on the right had stood for more than twenty years on what was once the front lawn of Tulse Dale.

Left: Mrs Patrick Campbell (1865–1940), Norwood's most distinguished actress, spent most of her early life in the district, and made her debut at the Institute in Chapel Road in 1886. The first of her many Norwood homes was Tulse Dale, which her mother looked after for a friend from 1874 to 1878.

Tulse Hill passes out of Norwood into Brixton at this crossroads. This is the view south towards Norwood Road, with Trinity Road (now Trinity Rise) on the left and Upper Tulse Hill on the right. The houses on the left, Ashurst Gardens, were built in about 1911 on the site of the large house called Ashurst Lodge.

Hillside Road was known as Trinity Road until 1886, which was confusing with another Trinity Road so close by. A change became essential when the first houses were built. There were four of them, all detached and all are still surviving. This was 2 Hillside Road, which has its entrance at the side in Lanercost Road.

This view of the junction where Norwood Road meets Tulse Hill and Thurlow Park Road has not changed much, except for the traffic, since 1911. The Tulse Hill Hotel, which was probably founded and built in 1846, is still trading, as are some of the 1870s shops beyond.

Until the 1880s there were few houses in Norwood Road north of the Tulse Hill Hotel. In the section adjoining Deronda Road, seen here in 1912, the houses on the right, backing onto the railway, were mostly built in 1881. The distinctive pairs on the left are conveniently dated '1885'. The shops beyond Deronda Road are a few years older.

Norwood Lodge, 323 Norwood Road, was one of a group of seven villas built in the 1860s between Thurlow Park Road and St Faith's Road, and today it is the best preserved of the ones that survive. This photograph was taken in 1908, when it was sent as a postcard by 'Ethel', probably one of the servants posing at the door. That was near the end of Norwood Lodge's career as a private house. Two years later it became the headquarters of the South London Botanical Institution, and that is still its use. The Institution had been founded in 1910 by Allan Octavian Hume (1829–1912), a distinguished civil servant and politician in India, where he was co-founder of the National Congress Party. On his return to England he devoted himself to his botanical and charitable interests. The South London Botanical Institution combined the two, as it was intended to 'convert the boy in the gutter to a love of British plants.' It did not achieve that ambition, but does continue as an active botanical club.

The triangular field on the west side of Norwood Road between the Tulse Hill Hotel and the Westmorland School was sold for development in the 1870s. Of the four new roads created, Romola, Deronda, and Deerbrook Roads are named after novels by George Eliot and Harriet Martineau, but Berwyn Road has no literary associations. The Edwardian postcards of Romola Road, above, and Deronda Road, show the houses built on the estate in the 1880s. In the Romola Road photograph the view is towards Deronda Road, with the spire of Holy Trinity beyond. The Deronda Road photographer was looking up from the corner of Deerbrook Road. Northcroft is now 33a Deronda Road.

The Westmorland Society's School in Norwood Road was built in 1853, when this was still almost the countryside and the Norwood hills could give the exiled pupils some faint reminder of the landscape of their distant county. It was a charity intended for the children of Westmorland parents living in or around London, where the society had been established in 1746, and there were generally twenty to thirty boarders, more boys than girls. The large grounds ran up the hill between Deronda Road and Trinity Rise to the garden of Silwood in Tulse Hill (now the St-Martin-in-the-Fields High School) and included what must have been a challengingly tilted cricket pitch. Demand for places fell throughout the history of the school, and it closed in the early 1920s. The St-Martin-in-the-Fields School acquired the playing fields. A garage was built in the front garden, so thriftily planted with vegetables when this Edwardian photograph was taken, and the last master and mistress of the school, James Hamilton and his wife, turned the main building into 'the Hamilton Trading Company, government contractors, Westmorland House'. The old school survived, hidden behind the garage, until after the Second World War, but the flats known as Sentamu Close have now been built on the site.

The Norwood countryside was a fading memory when this photograph was taken in the early 1920s. Buses and trams clattered along Norwood Road, and the gaunt 1880s houses on the left, opposite Trinity Rise, masked the railway line from Herne Hill to Tulse Hill. This part of Norwood Road had been widened for the trams, costing the Westmorland School part of its front garden.

Norwood ends at Trinity Rise, which was known until 1914 as Trinity Road. The south side was developed first. Houses began to appear there not long after Holy Trinity Church was completed in 1856. The north side, where the two ladies are walking in this 1920s photograph, was an open field until about 1910.

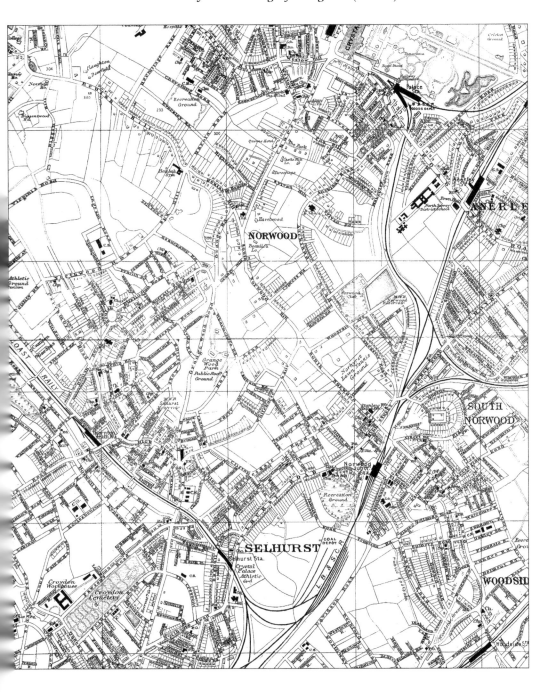

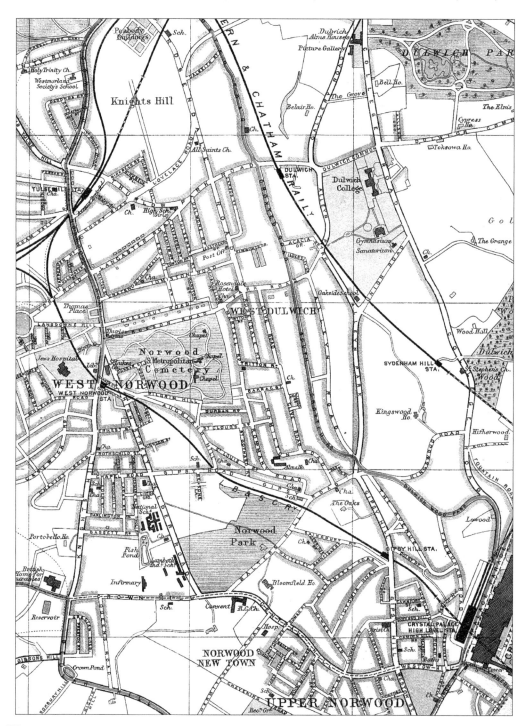

INDEX TO MAIN SUBJECTS